WAR W

CW00486133

Stop Line

by Major M. Green

Published by
REARDON PUBLISHING
56 Upper Norwood Street, Leckhampton
Cheltenham, Glos, GL53 0DU.
Website: www.reardon.co.uk

Copyright © 1999
Reardon Publishing

Written and Compiled
by
Major M. Green

Layout and Design
by
Nicholas Reardon

ISBN 1 873877 39 0

Photographs
by
J. Plant

Cover Design and illustration
by
Peter Reardon

Printed
by
IN2PRINT Ltd
Cheltenham

Part One
HISTORICAL BACKGROUND

By the autumn of 1939 during the early stages of the Second World War it became clear that German territorial ambitions extended to the conquest of all Western Europe. Great Britain therefore contributed an Expeditionary Force which was deployed on the Franco Belgian border to assist the Continental countries opposed to Germany. On 9th May 1940 Germany simultaneously invaded France, Holland and Belgium. By 2nd June 1940 the last members of the routed British Expeditionary Force (BEF) were evacuated back to England from the French port of Dunkirk. By 25th June France had surrendered and the German conquest was complete. The key ingredient to this extraordinary feat of arms was the German use of battle tanks which provided fire power, mobility and protection to their crews. The tanks were thus able to outflank and surround defending forces while destroying the command and support elements behind the lines held by those forces. It was a stated German aim that Great Britain should also be invaded. The threat was clear and taken entirely seriously after the humiliation of the BEF. Some kind of military counter to German armoured forces was required.

THE BRITISH MILITARY SOLUTION

Military planners realised that limiting the advantages enjoyed by attacking tanks was crucial to a successful defensive land battle in Britain. It was also realised that the best anti tank weapon was another tank, failing that an anti tank gun, but very small numbers of these types of equipment were available. It was, however, possible to limit enemy tank mobility by exploiting existing features such as rivers, canals, railway embankments and cuttings and creating artificial obstacles in the form of ditches and concrete bollards. This would at least prevent German tanks advancing without any hindrance at all and once halted, even if only temporarily, they could be counter attacked by some of the limited numbers of British tanks which could move to that specific point. This defensive tactic was adopted and a network of lines was developed all over England to stop tanks. They were called 'stop lines' and some were given colour code names.

STOP LINE GREEN

Stop Line Green (SLG) was a continuous linear defensive position some 100 miles long running in a rough semi circle east of Bristol from Highbridge on the Bristol Channel in the south to Upper Framilode on the River Severn in the north. Stop Line Green was also known as the Bristol Outer Defences. The detailed route of SLG was decided after a military reconnaissance in early June 1940. The report on that reconnaissance is at Part Two.

SLG was a last ditch position against an attack from the east and was built on the assumption that the Germans had already advanced this far west from the east or south coasts. Defending Bristol might keep the port open for evacuation purposes or resupply and reinforcement of the defenders.

There are junction points on SLG with Stop Line Yellow at Freshford near Bradford On Avon, Stop Line Blue at Whaddon near Melksham and Stop Line Red at Great Somerford near Malmesbury. All the stop lines were built in frantic haste since the invasion was considered as imminent. Work on them was halted in October 1940. By then the Royal Air Force had won the Battle of Britain in the air which made a German invasion impossible.

SURVIVING DEFENCE WORKS

An enormous amount of what was built and dug on SLG still exists. It is listed at Part Three. Much is of fine workmanship and in good condition. Most obvious are the block houses known as 'pill boxes'. They are sited on the edge of or very close to the obstacle intended to stop tanks and made of steel reinforced concrete cast in wood, brick, prefabricated or corrugated asbestos shuttering. Those on SLG were to be manned by infantry equipped with small arms and comprise two basic designs known as the Type 26, see page 22, and the Type 29, see page 23. The Type 26 is square, Photographs 1 and 2, and the Type 29 is hexagonal, Photographs 3, 4 and 5. Within each type on SLG there is considerable variety in the detail of dimensions - wall and roof thickness, height above ground, size of firing ports, width of door or porch, length of external walls ...... etc. This is because many different local firms were contracted to build them who followed the War Office specifications with varying degrees of accuracy.

The main artificial tank stopping obstacle was a ditch anything up to 12 feet deep and 20 feet wide, Photograph 6, dug by bull dozers and drag line excavators assisted in some places by explosives. It was commonly known as a 'tank trap' and was usually continued straight across minor roads where makeshift wooden bridges were provided which were to be removed as the enemy approached. Very little unfilled tank trap remains but much was refilled without separating stone from top soil leaving a characteristic hump, Photograph 7.

There are rectangular and tubular anti tank bollards, Photograph 8, prefabricated or cast in situ in wood, corrugated iron and water main pipe shuttering. Some were put in the stop line proper and some were placed ready to block roads and bridges over the line or to act as anchors for welded together jumbles of railway tracks to be dropped onto such crossing points. Certain bridges were prepared for demolition, so that the enemy could not use them, by drilling holes for explosive charges which were to be laid and fired at an appropriate moment. This was the case at River Bridge, Mark Moor and Cowbridge, Malmesbury.

MILITARY UTILITY

SLG was not tested in battle so only tentative comments are possible. It suffers from the disadvantage common to all linear defence that a penetration at one point compromises the whole position. The tank stopping obstacles - rivers, railway cuttings, canals, bollards, tank trap ...... etc would hinder advancing tanks, then and now, until field engineers made a crossing through or over them. The delay imposed even in 1940 would have been brief because the Germans had such engineers in their forward combat formations. SLG could not have been held unless tanks halted anywhere along it were counter attacked and destroyed or driven back within a very few hours of their arrival. Having already lost the defensive battle this far north and west counter attack forces, especially tanks, would probably have been scarce. However, in this desperate situation SLG would at least have been an immediately identifiable rallying point for forces withdrawing from the occupied areas. Some 1941 pill box training notes are on the rear cover. All those on SLG are proof against small arms and the Type 29's are proof against the German tank guns of the time. All would have provided good protection from anything short of a direct hit or very near miss by the bombs or field artillery then available but they have no anti tank function. They pose a serious threat to attacking enemy infantry but a few hits on the outside from the guns of attacking tanks would quickly disorientate those inside and reduce their fighting efficiency. The pill boxes are large, obvious, easy targets. Most are mounted on a concrete base and stand up to 8 feet tall. The air field defence pill box at Kemble near Cirencester, Photograph 9, is much more difficult to hit. All bar the top 2 feet 4 inches, firing ports and a headspace for the defenders, is below ground level. Very few SLG pill boxes are 'dug in' like this to reduce their target size and visibility.

Stop Lines Red and Blue include pill boxes known as the Type 28, Photograph 10, designed to house the Two Pounder anti tank gun, a weapon lethal to the German tanks of the time. There are no Type 28 pill boxes on SLG. This may be a tacit admission that all the Two Pounders would have been lost in action by the time the enemy reached SLG. Some respected historians say there were anyway less than 200 in the whole country in July 1940.

Stop lines may have been intended to deter an invasion. Their existence would have been obvious to enemy air reconnaissance. A further intention might have been to convince the United States of Great Britain's plight and encourage intervention on her behalf. They might also have been meant to impress on the British public the danger which faced them and stiffen their will to resist. Certainly Winston Churchill was determined that national opposition to an invasion would not collapse as it had on the Continent. It was ultimately his decision that the stop lines should be constructed.

CONCLUSION

Stop Line Green is today a remarkably complete and very well preserved specimen of military archaeology. It is emphatic historical evidence of how seriously the threat of a German invasion was taken. The line is frequently crossed and followed by public foot paths so can be easily visited. Some suggested walks are at Part Four which are best done in winter when the vegetation has died back so that the defence works are not obscured. A torch, Wellington boots and binoculars are essential equipment. A significant change to the country side is the wholesale amalgamation of small enclosures in the 1960's, when many miles of hedge and wall were removed, which has made the approaches to SLG favourable to the attacker. It is now good tank country offering easy passage with wide and deep fields of view and fire. In 1940 the land use was much more favourable to the defender.

Part Two
RECONNAISSANCE REPORT ON BRISTOL OUTER DEFENCES
DATED 18TH JUNE 1940

GENERAL DESCRIPTION

The right flank of the position rests on the BRISTOL CHANNEL at HIGHBRIDGE. The Forward Defence Line (FDL) follows the RIVER BRUE and tributaries as far as a point 1 mile south east of WELLS. From there it crosses the MENDIP PLATEAU to MASBURY STATION. There is no natural obstacle across the plateau. From MASBURY to RADSTOCK the line of the Somerset & Dorset Railway is followed and thence the line of the WELLOW BROOK to the RIVER AVON at BRADFORD ON AVON.

From BRADFORD ON AVON the AVON is followed upstream to MALMESBURY where the river ceases to be an effective anti tank obstacle. From this point to NAILSWORTH the position crosses the COTSWOLD PLATEAU. In this sector also there is no natural obstacle and an artificial ditch should be dug. It is, however, doubtful whether the excavators will be able to work in this lime stone belt owing to very little depth of surface earth. This will have to be verified by local reconnaissance.

From NAILSWORTH to STROUD the position is sited behind the gorge and water course between these two places and from STROUD to the RIVER SEVERN the FDL follows the line of the RIVER FROME and the STROUD WATER CANAL.

The position is strong on the south west and north east flanks and from BRADFORD ON AVON to just below MALMESBURY. The weaker sectors are from WELLS to BRADFORD ON AVON and from MALMESBURY to NAILSWORTH where either no natural obstacle exists or the natural obstacle is only partial. At LACOCK the position is badly overlooked from the east.

A great deal depends on whether the excavators can work in the lime stone country. If they can there should be no difficulty in creating a continuous obstacle against tanks along the forward edge of the position.

DETAILED DESCRIPTION

Highbridge to Wells

From the sea to MEARE POOL the RIVER BRUE forms an effective obstacle being wide, deep, muddy and with vertical banks.

From MEARE POOL to UPPER GODNEY the RIVER SHEPPEY is also an effective obstacle. From UPPER GODNEY to DINDER the above river is only a partial obstacle and improvement will be necessary.

Dinder to Radstock

From DINDER to MASBURY STATION the FDL is sited along the south east face of DINDER WOOD and thence up the spur to MASBURY STATION. An artificial obstacle will be required.

From MASBURY STATION to RADSTOCK the Somerset and Dorset Railway is followed. Although the line of the railway is not always sited suitably from a tactical point of view the cuttings and embankments on it, being cut out of limestone, are very steep and provide complete anti tank protection where they exist

Radstock to Freshford

From RADSTOCK the FDL follows the general line of the WELLOW BROOK as far as the re-entrant at MIDFORD HILL. As an obstacle the WELLOW BROOK depends on its banks which are overgrown and at least partially effective.

From MIDFORD HILL the FDL passes across the LIMPLEY STOKE tongue and drops to the AVON VALLEY and FRESHFORD. An artificial obstacle will be required in this sector.

Freshford to Malmesbury

The line of the RIVER AVON is followed. This is a complete anti tank obstacle as far upstream as CHIPPENHAM after which it can not be relied on and local improvement may be necessary.

There is an unsatisfactory sector near LACOCK where the position is badly overlooked from the high ground at BOWDEN PARK.

In the sector from GREAT SOMERFORD to MALMESBURY the RIVER AVON is often wide, swift and shallow with indifferent banks and a hard bottom so it can not be relied on as an anti tank obstacle.

Malmesbury to Nailsworth

From MALMESBURY the FDL leaves the AVON and runs north and north west over the COTSWOLD PLATEAU making use of the best tactical ground. The position includes WARREN TUMP and STAR FARM and drops into the NAILSWORTH GORGE at AVENING.

This is a weak sector from the point of view of anti tank defence and an artificial ditch should be constructed if the excavators are capable of working the ground which is limestone thinly covered with earth.

From AVENING to NAILSWORTH the gorge is steep and is itself a complete anti tank obstacle.

Nailsworth to the River Severn

As far as DUDBRIDGE the NAILSWORTH GORGE is a complete anti tank obstacle and from DUDBRIDGE to the RIVER SEVERN the line of the STROUD WATER CANAL also provides complete protection. This sector should not absorb many troops.

REVIEW OF RECONNAISSANCE REPORT ON BRISTOL OUTER DEFENCES DATED 7TH JULY 1940

GENERAL

The reviewers agree with the Reconnaissance Report with the following exceptions :

(a) As the stream from LOWER GODNEY to UPPER GODNEY (River Sheppey) is a poor obstacle the line will now follow the DIVISION RHYNE from MEARE POOL, thence an artificial obstacle must be constructed. (See Note 1)

(b) The task of constructing an artificial obstacle across the COTSWOLD PLATEAU in the MALMESBURY - AVENING sector is a difficult one owing to the hardness of the ground. In order to take advantage of a natural anti tank obstacle the line will now run further west along the RIVER AVON (Tetbury Branch) as far as ESCOURT HOUSE, then TETBURY, thence to AVENING. (See Note 2)

THE OBSTACLE

Further detailed reconnaissances have confirmed your report in general but considerable work will be required to improve the obstacle by building up the banks of rivers and streams. It is not agreed the the gorge between AVENING and DUDBRIDGE is an obstacle to tanks although it will undoubtedly slow them up.

TROOPS REQUIRED

In considering the number of Divisions required to hold the line 8000 yards has been taken as an average Divisional frontage. This is, of course, too wide to repel serious attacks for any length of time.

The country is very enclosed except across the COTSWOLD PLATEAU and in parts of the sector MASBURY to RADSTOCK. It is therefore expensive in troops even by day, particularly where the country is dead flat and there is no observation beyond the obstacle, such as the sector HIGHBRIDGE to DINDER. In other parts of the line although the country is enclosed it is hilly and better observation is obtained. These factors have been taken into consideration when selecting Divisional Boundaries. Sixteen Divisions will be required if the whole line is to be held.

Note 1. In the event it seems that both obstacles were in fact used. Defence Works 42 and 43 conform to the River Sheppey. Defence Works 40 and 41 conform to this revision.

Note 2. This revision,although there is much to be said for it,was not taken up. The line was built to swing north, away from the Avon, on the east side of Malmesbury. Local memory records that work on the tank trap was already well under way by 7th July 1940.

Part Three
SURVIVING DEFENCE WORKS

No.	GRID REF	DESCRIPTION	PLACE NAME
1	30354737	Type 29 pill box	Mouth of River Brue
2	32184701	Type 29 pill box	Highbridge Railway Station
3	32204672	Type 29 pill box	Brue Farm
3a	32884623	Type 29 pill box	M5 Overbridge
4	33494621	Type 29 pill box	West Hill Farm
5	33684600	Type 29 pill box	West Hill Farm
6	34014589	Type 29 pill box	Churchland Farm
6a	34424585	Type 29 pill box	Bason Bridge
7	34904573	Type 29 pill box	Moor Row,Bason Bridge
8	35544544	Type 29 pill box	Mark Moor
9	35894529	Type 29 pill box	Mark Moor
10	36074522	Type 29 pill box	Cripps Bridge,Mark Moor
11	36214523	Type 29 pill box	Cripps Bridge,Mark Moor
12	36484519	Type 29 pill box	Mark Moor
13	36664515	Type 29 pill box	Mark Moor
14	36834514	Type 29 pill box	Mark Moor
15	37294510	Type 29 pill box	Mark Moor
16	37424504	Type 29 pill box	Mark Moor
17	37674498	Type 29 pill box	Mark Moor
18	37794492	Type 29 pill box	Mark Moor
19	37894481	Type 29 pill box	Mark Moor
20	38034466	Type 29 pill box	Riverside Farm
21	38154460	Type 29 pill box	River Bridge
22	38334464	Type 29 pill box	Orchard Farm
23	38934480	2 anti tank bollards	River House Farm
24	39064479	Type 29 pill box	River House Farm
25	39314483	Type 29 pill box	River House Farm
26	39774485	Type 29 pill box	Watt's Lane Pump House
27	40204470	Type 29 pill box	Tadham Moor
28	40514452	Type 29 pill box	Tadham Moor
29	41054430	Type 29 pill box	Tadham Moor
30	41434405	Type 29 pill box	Tadham Moor
31	41804379	Type 29 pill box	Tadham Moor
32	42114360	Type 29 pill box	Tadham Moor
33	42474340	Type 29 pill box	Tadham Moor
34	42814322	Type 29 pill box	Tadham Moor
35	43444282	Type 29 pill box	Westhay
36	44014259	Type 29 pill box	Westhay
37	44354262	Type 29 pill box	Westhay

Photo No.1 Type 26 Pill Box at Lackham

Photo No. 2. Type 26 Pill Box at Long Newnton

Photo No.3 Type 29 Pill Box at Stony Littleton

Photo No.4 Type 29 Pill Box at Staverton

38	44994249	Type 29 pill box	White's River
39	45794231	Type 29 pill box	Meare Pool,Division Rhyne
40	48154207	Type 29 pill box	Division Rhyne
41	48614215	Type 29 pill box	Division Rhyne Bridge
42	49104289	Type 29 pill box	Upper Godney
43	49204280	Type 29 pill box	Upper Godney
44	49194273	3 anti tank bollards	Upper Godney
44a	49174268	10 anti tank bollards	Higher Bridge Farm
45	50374339	Type 29 pill box	North Moor
46	52364344	Type 29 pill box	Coxley Railway Bridge
47	52604366	Type 29 pill box	Wick Farm
48	52884382	7 anti tank bollards	Coxley Playing Field
49	53834408	5 anti tank bollards	Woodford Bridge
50	54064418	25 anti tank bollards	Woodford Farm Bridge
51	55984545	Type 29 pill box	Constitution Hill
52	56154547	Type 29 pill box	Constitution Hill
52a	56194552	35 anti tank bollards	Torhill Quarry
53	56284532	Type 29 pill box	Constitution Hill
54	56644529	Type 29 pill box	Colver's Brow
55	57014540	Type 29 pill box	Steep Holme
56	57184528	Type 29 pill box	Steep Holme
57	57524530	28 anti tank bollards	Sharcombe Park
58	57604520	Type 29 pill box	Sharcombe Park
59	58004507	Type 29 pill box	Dinder Wood
60	58424539	Type 29 pill box	Furzy Sleight
60a	58834543	20+ anti tank bollards	Dinder Wood
61	58934559	Type 29 pill box	Chilcote Lane
62	58844599	Type 29 pill box	Five Acre Wood
63	58904609	Unfilled tank trap	Five Acre Wood
64	58934619	Type 29 pill box	Five Acre Wood
65	59214643	Type 29 pill box	Pitts Wood
66	59334650	Tank trap hump	Pitts Farm
67	60024690	Type 29 pill box	Spring Wood
68	60394693	Type 29 pill box	Spring Wood
69	60454690	Unfilled tank trap	Masbury
70	60584688	3 anti tank bollards	Thrupe Lane
70a	61034812	Type 29 pill box	Railway Bridge
71	61044851	Type 29 pill box	Whitnell House Farm
72	61484910	Type 29 pill box	Binegar Station
73	61704929	Type 26 pill box	Binegar Bridge (site of)
74	62134989	Type 29 pill box	Tellis Lane
75	62145004	Type 29 pill box	Portway Lane
76	62035034	Type 29 pill box	Emborough Quarries
77	62255080	2 anti tank bollards	Emborough Quarries

78	62585091	Type 26 pill box	Marchant's Hill
79	62685095 to	84 anti tank bollards	
	62995106	and unfilled tank trap	Old Down
80	62995101	Type 26 pill box	Coal Pit Lane
81	63185123	Type 29 pill box	Old Down Mound
82	64905147	6 anti tank bollards	Fry's Well Bridge
83	64965150	Type 29 pill box	Fry's Well Bridge
84	65275219	Type 29 pill box	Tunnel Lane
85	65295239	Type 29 pill box	Tunnel Lane
86	66265344	Type 29 pill box	Midsomer Norton Station
87	66395360	Type 29 pill box	Midsomer Norton Station
87a	68415449	Type 29 pill box	Dring Lane
87b	68575458	Type 29 pill box	College Boundary
87c	68705462	Type 29 pill box	College Boundary
88	67915470	1 anti tank bollard	Fosse Cottage,Radstock
89	70505542	Type 29 pill box	Lower Writhlington Colliery
90	70695551	Type 29 pill box	Braysdown Lane
91	70765544	Type 29 pill box	Lower Writhlington Siding
92	70895553	Type 29 pill box	Lower Writhlington Siding
93	71065565	Type 29 pill box	Paglinch Farm
94	71215575	Type 29 pill box	Paglinch Farm
95	71715591	Type 29 pill box	Shoscombe Vale
96	71885606	Type 29 pill box	Shoscombe Vale
97	72065618	5 anti tank bollards	Single Hill Bridge
98	72905648	5 anti tank bollards	Stony Littleton
99	72845654	Type 29 pill box	Stony Littleton
100	73085672	6 anti tank bollards	Stony Littleton
101	73335675	3 anti tank bollards	Stony Littleton
102	73315685	Type 29 pill box	Green Acres Farm
103	73595770	Type 29 pill box	Willow Farm
104	74285805	Type 29 pill box	Church Farm
105	74585811	Type 29 pill box	Church Farm
106	75085825	Type 29 pill box	Hinton Hill
106a	75195824	Type 26 pill box	Hinton Hill
107	75415842	Type 29 pill box	Hankley Bottom
108	75795902	Type 29 pill box	Twinhoeford
109	75805935	Type 29 pill box	Twinhoeford
110	75935950	Type 29 pill box	Twinhoeford
111	76315962	Type 26 pill box	Midford Valley
112	76395960	Type 29 pill box	Midford Valley
113	76725935	Type 29 pill box	Hang Wood
114	77025950	Type 29 pill box	Midford Hill
115	77225955	Type 26 pill box	Hog Wood
116	77415944	Type 29 pill box	Hog Wood

Photo No.5 Type 29 Pill Box at Lacock

Photo No.6 Unfilled Tank Trap at Hinton Charterhouse

Photo No.7 Tank Trap Hump at Avening

Photo No.8 Anti Tank Bollards at Stony Littleton

117	77515952	Type 29 pill box	Hog Wood
118	77225955 to		
	77515952	Unfilled tank trap	Hog Wood
119	77515952 to		
	77455956	Unfilled infantry trenches	Hog Wood
120	78335950	Type 29 pill box	Pond House
120a	78315967	Type 29 pill box	Sharpstone
120b	78565951	Type 29 pill box	Sharpstone
121	78645974	Type 29 pill box	Freshford Mill Bridge
122	78915990	Type 29 pill box	Woodside
123	79145992	Type 29 pill box	Woodside Bridge
124	79416008	Type 29 pill box	Freshford Railway Bridge
125	79995990	Type 29 pill box	Avoncliff
126	80396012	Type 26 pill box	Avoncliff
127	82306052	Type 29 pill box	Bradford Tithe Barn Bridge
128	82316062	4 anti tank bollards	Bradford on Avon Station
129	82645979	Type 26 pill box	Kennet Avon Canal
130	82936070	Type 26 pill box	Bradford on Avon Weir
131	84006029	Type 29 pill box	Hall Estate
132	84445988	Type 29 pill box	Hall Estate
133	84535994	Type 29 pill box	Hall Estate
134	85056002	Type 29 pill box	Bradford Junctions Bridge
135	85056004	Type 29 pill box	Bradford Junctions Bridge
136	84866075	Type 29 pill box	Great Bradford Wood
137	85136110	Type 29 pill box	Forewoods Common
138	85606119	Type 29 pill box	Manor Farm
139	86026118	Type 29 pill box	Staverton Weir
140	86346112	Type 29 pill box	Staverton Weir Railway Bridge
141	86386126	Type 29 pill box	Avon View Farm
142	86646127	Type 29 pill box	Holt Level Crossing
143	87006148	Type 29 pill box	Holt Halt (site of)
144	87446175	Type 29 pill box	Holt Junction (site of)
145	87606179	Type 29 pill box	Holt Junction (site of)
146	88056172	Type 29 pill box	Whaddon Railway Bridge (site of)
147	88166174	Type 29 pill box	Whaddon Railway Bridge (site of)
148	88206217	Type 29 pill box	Pack Horse Bridge
149	88426234	Type 29 pill box	Monkton House
150	88726238	Type 29 pill box	Red House Farm
151	89066284	Type 29 pill box	Red House Farm
152	89326345	Type 29 pill box	Red House Farm
153	89476360	Type 29 pill box	Challeymead

154	90676535	Type 29 pill box	Half Way Farm
155	90466572	Type 29 pill box	Beechfield House
156	91636738	Type 29 pill box	Riverside
157	91876763	Type 29 pill box	Lacock Sewage Works
158	92106807	Type 29 pill box	Lacock Bridge
159	92006874	Type 29 pill box	Lacock Abbey Weir
160	92366964	Type 29 pill box	Lackham Wood
161	92926995	Type 29 pill box	Lackham Wood
162	93057006	Type 29 pill box	Lackham Wood
163	92897030	Type 29 pill box	North Wood
164	91507025	Type 29 pill box	Lodge Wood
165	91707035	Type 26 pill box	Plucking Grove
166	91557134	Type 29 pill box	Milbourne Farm
167	91917189	Type 29 pill box	Rowden Farm
168	91867250	Type 29 pill box	Rowden Farm
169	92427347	Type 29 pill box	28 Sadlers Mead, Chippenham
170	92647313	Type 29 pill box	Monkton Park
171	93327379	Type 29 pill box	Cocklebury Railway Bridge (site of)
172	95997831	Type 29 pill box	Christian Malford
173	95747861	Type 29 pill box	Sutton Benger
174	95287896	Type 29 pill box	Sutton Benger
175	94987940	Type 29 pill box	Brookside
176	97638205	Type 29 pill box	Dauntsey Lower Weir
177	97238251	Type 29 pill box	Dauntsey Level Crossing
178	98078396	Type 29 pill box	Somerford Bridge
179	96628320	Type 29 pill box	Brook Farm
180	96368319	Type 29 pill box	Brook Farm
181	95718420	Type 29 pill box	Kings Mead
182	94638557	Type 29 pill box	Cole Park Farm
183	94188614	21 anti tank bollards	Cowbridge Ford
184	94338625	Type 29 pill box	Cowbridge
185	93978648	Type 29 pill box	Burton Hill
186	94318670	Type 26 pill box	Cowbridge Farm
187	94308689	River bank revetting	Cowbridge Farm
188	93528873	Type 26 pill box	Filands Farm
189	93188894	Type 26 pill box	White Lodge Farm
190	92748930	Type 29 pill box	Quobwell Farm
191	92449001	Type 29 pill box	Quobwell Plantations
192	92509025	Type 29 pill box	Quobwell Plantations
193	92479030	Type 26 pill box	Coldharbour Hill
194	92489060	Type 26 pill box	Coldharbour Wood
195	92509090	Type 29 pill box	Gilboa Farm

Photo No.9 Kemble Aerodrome Pill Box

Photo No.10 Type 28 Pill Box at Whaddon

Photo No.11 River bank revetting at Malmesbury

Photo No.12 Type 29 Pill Box at Hinton Charterhouse

196	92559109	Type 29 pill box	Gilboa Farm
197	92179154	1 anti tank bollard	Long Newnton Aerodrome
198	91859140	Type 26 pill box	Fosse Way
199	91759147	Type 26 pill box	Fosse Way
200	91799178 to		
	91859215	Tank trap hump	Aerodrome Farm
201	91879198	Type 29 pill box	Aerodrome Farm
202	91709269	Type 29 pill box	Church Farm
203	91429319	Type 29 pill box	Church Farm
204	91189341	Type 29 pill box	Church Farm
205	90959347	Type 29 pill box	Little Lark Hill Farm
206	90659405	16 anti tank bollards	Little Lark Hill Farm
207	90509410	8 anti tank bollards	Tetbury Branch Line
208	90339510	Tank trap hump	Broadfield Farm
209	90549567 to		
	90459580	Tank trap hump	Warren Farm
210	90209609	Type 29 pill box	Pimbury Park
211	90209609 to		
	90069638	Tank trap hump	Pimbury Park
212	89799652	Type 29 pill box	Star Lane
213	89319694 to		
	89189692	Unfilled tank trap	Star Farm
214	88959712	Type 29 pill box	Star Farm Cottages
215	88869724 to		
	88789762	Tank trap hump	Star Lane
216	88709773	Type 29 pill box	Star Lane
217	88679774	4 anti tank bollards	Star Lane
218	78060565	Type 29 pill box	Meadow Bridge
219	78310609	Type 29 pill box	Stroud Water Canal Locks
220	77100733	Type 29 pill box	Frome Bridge
221	77210748	Type 29 pill box	Wharf
222	76580832	Type 26 pill box	Stone Pitts
223	75650938	Type 26 pill box	Junction Bridge
224	75231009	Type 29 pill box	Upper Framilode
225	69831190	Type 26 pill box	Arlingham Passage
226	69391048	Type 26 pill box	Arlingham Passage

DEFENCE WORKS	MAP SHEET
1 to 26	Explorer 22
27 to 66	Explorer 141
67 to 124	Explorer 142
125 to 177	Explorer 156
178 to 219	Explorer 168
220 to 226	Outdoor Leisure 14

TYPE 26 PILL BOX

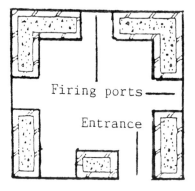

Firing ports

Entrance

Viewed from above, roof cut away.
Walls up to 21 inches thick,
external length 10 feet by 10 feet

TYPE 28 PILL BOX

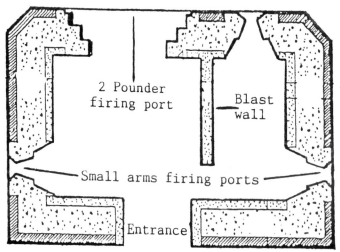

2 Pounder
firing port

Blast
wall

Small arms firing ports

Entrance

Viewed from above, roof cut away.
Walls up to 50 inches thick,
external length 28 feet by 20 feet

TYPE 29 PILL BOX

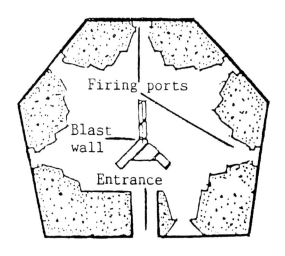

Firing ports

Blast wall

Entrance

Viewed from above, roof cut away.
Walls up to 47 inches thick,
external lengths - three at 9 feet 4 inches,
two at 11 feet,
one at 17 feet 8 inches

Part Four
RECOMMENDED WALKS

WESTHAY, NEAR WEDMORE, SOMERSET
Distance to walk : 5 miles
Ordnance Survey Map Sheet Explorer 141

Approach Westhay from Wedmore on the B3151. There is a tarmac parking place on the right side of the road just short of the bridge over the River Brue on the Wedmore side of Westhay. Follow the stone track from the parking place towards the river for about 40 yards then turn right through the gate into the field. You are now on a public foot path which runs along the bank of the River Brue for the first 2 miles of the walk.

It will take you past 7 Type 29 pill boxes placed to face an enemy on the far side of the river. They are defence works 29 to 35 in Part Three. All are constructed with red brick shuttering and show the typical lay out of SLG with pill boxes perched on the edge of the anti tank obstacle which in this case is the River Brue itself. The river is just as good an obstacle now as it was noted to be by the military planners in June 1940, see Part Two. Some of the pill boxes look well dug in but this is because spoil dredged from the river since 1940 has been banked up against the walls. The sixth one reached was built to a very high standard and is clean, dry and little affected by over half a century of exposure to the weather. The fields over the river opposite to the seventh pill box are unchanged in size and shape since 1940. They show what difficult tank country all this part of Somerset was at that time because the thick hedges and deep ditches limited mobility and it was only possible to see, and therefore shoot, from hedge to hedge which was often less than 100 yards.

Having gone through the gate immediately after pill box 7 turn right along the bank of the deep drainage ditch which is called Bounds Rhyne. The foot path follows Bounds Rhyne for the next half mile to the single track lane called Totney Drove, a public road. Turn right onto Totney Drove and follow it to the junction with the B3151. Turn right onto the B3151 and follow this road for 1 mile back to the start point. There is one sharp left hand bend and as you approach the subsequent sharp right hand bend at the Turnpike House Mr Sweet's Peat and Science Museum is on the left side. The museum contains the remains of a Junkers 88 which was shot down and crashed by the junction of Totney Drove and the B3151 in 1944 after it had bombed Bristol. It can be viewed by appointment with Mr Sweet whose telephone number is 01 458 860650. During the last 100 yards to the parking place another Type 29 is visible across the field on the left beside the river. It uses precast concrete blocks as shuttering and can be reached by the river bank footpath.

DULCOTE, NEAR WELLS, SOMERSET
Distance to walk : 2 and 1/2 miles
Ordnance Survey Map Sheet Explorer 141

Approach Dulcote from Wells on the A371. Half a mile after the built up area of Wells ends the road reaches the crest of Constitution Hill. Half way down on the right hand side is a gravel surfaced parking place surrounded by beech trees. Opposite to it on the far side of the road is a kissing gate. Go through it and you are on a circuit past defence works 51 to 58 in Part Three placed to face an enemy advancing from the valley at the bottom of Constitution Hill. They are are 7 red brick shuttered Type 29 pill boxes and a substantial group of anti tank bollards. From the kissing gate a well signed public foot path through 6 fields and a cricket ground runs directly to Saint Michael and All Angels Church at Dinder, the tower of which is always in sight.

The first pill box is visible half left immediately on leaving the A371 at the junction of the first two fields and the wood. The second appears,again half left,below the tree line once the sunken lane between the second and third field has been crossed. The tank stopping obstacle here was a tank trap. When the grass is eaten off short or mown for hay/silage a slight hump where the tank trap was filled in is just visible running across the slope in front of this second pill box. In Part Two, the military report on SLG dated 18th June 1940, the author notes that the line is badly 'overlooked' near Lacock. He means that the hills on the 'enemy' side of the defence line offer a complete view over it so that a German artillery observer on them would be invulnerable as he directed fire onto the defenders. Precisely this criticism also applies here. Dulcote Hill on the right towers above this section of the walk.

From the kissing gate between the fourth and fifth fields a third pill box is visible half left in the very edge of the tree line. The foot path now leads round,not over,the cricket ground into Dead End Lane. Turn left on this public road and take the first left, another tarmac public road, opposite the gate into the church yard. This lane leads past Dinder village hall on the left and the wrought iron ornamental gates into Sharcombe Park on the right. At the foot of the wooded hills, the tarmac has by now been replaced by cobbles, take the sharp left, also a cobbled track, through the gateway. The fourth pill box is immediately on the left. As the track climbs the hill a total of 28 large rectangular anti tank bollards are spread out on either side. The track runs into a field and the public path continues parallel with the woods on the left through a hunt gate on the far side of the field into the woods themselves. Where it turns sharp right the fifth pill box is visible during the winter months through the trees down the slope on the left. It is unusual in having an entrance porch running along most of the rear wall. After the next hunt gate turn left. The track is now stone surfaced again and runs parallel with a golf course on the left. Opposite the first private house on the right is a stile in the hedge on the left. Once over it the sixth pill box is on the crest of the hill on the right. It demonstrates the field of view available to troops manning the Type 29. It also demonstrates what large,obvious targets pill boxes can be. The public path can be followed straight down hill from the stile. It leads to the kissing gate opposite the parking place. Alternately the stone track can be rejoined and followed until it meets the A371 at the top of Constitution Hill. Where it does so there is a private house on the left with the seventh pill box in the grounds. It is used as a wood shed. It fronts the road and was probably sited to cover that as it has no field of fire over the stop line itself. The internal blast wall has been removed to make more room. Turn left on the A371 to regain the parking place.

LOWER WRITHLINGTON, NEAR RADSTOCK, SOMERSET
Distance to walk : 2 miles
Ordnance Survey Map Sheet Explorer 142

Take the A362 road from Radstock to Frome and at the top of the hill out of Radstock turn sharp left at the Hayloft Inn. You are now on Church Hill which will lead you to the bottom of the valley through which runs the Wellow Brook and the old Somerset & Dorset railway line. Soon after passing the redundant church on the left a lane merges from the right and a level area of waste land appears on the left. It was a storage area for the abandoned Lower Writhlington Colliery and the concrete gateway is a suitable place to park. Continue on foot over the Wellow Brook bridge, under the railway bridge and for 80 yards up the lane at which point there is a gap in the low railway embankment on the right. Go through this gap and you are on a public foot path along the dismantled railway at the start of a circuit past defence works 90 to 94 in Part Three, 5 red brick shuttered Type 29 pill boxes placed to face an enemy from the far side of the River Wellow.

Once off the lane you are in what was a siding for coal loading, in full use during 1940. Turn left and walk along the right hand side of this open,level area. The first pill box, heavily overgrown, is on the top of the embankment leading down to the Wellow Brook. The path now climbs over a pile of rubble, the remains of railway buildings, from which the second pill box is visible, this time at the foot of the embankment. At this point in 1876 two trains collided head on and 13 people were killed, the Great Radstock Disaster. The railway now enters a cutting spanned by an iron bridge built to connect fields owned by the same farm but separated by the line, called an occupation bridge. Climb the cutting on the right hand side 30 yards short of the bridge, turn left and the third pill box, built into the dry stone wall at the entrance to the bridge, is visible. Merging it with the wall would have had some camouflage effect and it controls the bridge over the anti tank obstacle.

So far the pill boxes have been sited more to use the railway line than the Wellow Brook as the obstacle although the military planners, see Part Two, specified the latter. Now cross the iron bridge and turn right. The path, well signed, runs along the top of the cutting until it merges with the farm road leading into Paglinch Farm which is on the right. There is another pill box visible in the garden of Paglinch Farm. This one is sited to use the Wellow Brook as the anti tank obstacle. The farm road leads to the lane called Green Street. Turn right on Green Street, pass between the railway bridge buttresses, over the Wellow Brook and start the stiff climb up Foxcote Hill. At the 90 degree left hand bend climb the post and rail fence on the left side of the entrance to the house on the right. You are again on a public foot path, well signed and provided with stiles, which runs parallel to the Wellow Brook back towards Radstock through 3 fields, a wood and a field. Once through the wood the final pill box can be seen, only during the winter, on the hill side above, and thus covering, the railway bridge by the coal siding. The foot path joins Church Hill opposite to a stone pillar with a memorial plaque to George Fairfax. Turn right and the parking place is on the left.

STONY LITTLETON, NEAR RADSTOCK, SOMERSET
Distance to walk : 1 and 3/4 miles
Ordnance Survey Map Sheet Explorer 142

On the A366 road between Trowbridge and Radstock is the village of Faulkland. Turn into Grove Lane opposite the Faulkland Inn public house. You will travel down Lippiat Hill and Faulkland Lane to the valley bottom through which runs the Wellow Brook. 100 yards short of the bridge over Wellow Brook is a wide verge on the right on which to park.

Continue on foot over the Wellow Brook and take the first right which is a tarmac surfaced by way. You are now on the 'friendly' side of SLG at the start of a circuit past defence works 98 to 102 in Part Three, 2 red brick shuttered Type 29 pill boxes and 3 groups of anti tank bollards. The first pill box is visible at once on the left verge of the by way, Photograph 3. It is in fine condition mainly due to the builders adding a thin layer of concrete all over the roof to seal the gap between the shuttering bricks and the filling. There are the remains of hooks let into the bricks for the attachment of camouflage netting. Look right at the Wellow and the triangular tips of 5 anti tank bollards protrude out of the water. It is likely that they were placed to block what was a crossing point in 1940. This is common to the next two groups of bollards. In all three cases the brook has a firm bottom although the banks have become steep through erosion by the flowing water. A short distance further along the by way is a group of 6 rectangular bollards, Photograph 8. The road now curves right handed then left handed. There is a near vertical stone bank on the left. As this ends the second pill box comes into view in the field on the left. All the brick shuttering has fallen off it exposing the concrete filling and metal reinforcing rods. No doubt it was built to a lower standard than the first one. The final group of 3 anti tank bollards is also visible on the far side of the Wellow at this point. Turn right onto the English Heritage foot bridge over the Wellow opposite Greenacres Farm. You are now on a bridle path.

Make your way up hill to the derelict stone barn visible at the top. From it there is a good view back over the Wellow which is the anti tank obstacle. The line of trees across the forward slope on the other side of the valley marks the dismantled Somerset & Dorset Railway which was the anti tank obstacle further south, towards Radstock. Turn right at the barn and follow the bridle path through one gate and along a grass track up to the corner of Littleton Wood on your left. There is a cross tracks here at which turn right down the sunken lane and right again when it joins Faulkland Lane. Follow Faulkland Lane downhill back to the parking place.

HINTON CHARTERHOUSE, NEAR BATH, SOMERSET
Distance to walk : 1 and 1/4 miles
Ordnance Survey Map Sheet Explorer 142

Take the B3110 from Hinton Charterhouse towards Midford. 3/4 of a mile from Hinton Charterhouse is the crest of Midford Hill. As the road begins to descend there is a very sharp left hand bend. On the right is a broad area of tarmac on which to park. On the uphill side of this parking place is a wooden stile marked with a foot path arrow. It is the start of a circuit past defence works 115 to 119 in Part Three, a Type 26 and three Type 29 pill boxes, all red brick shuttered, a length of unfilled tank trap and some unfilled infantry trenches.

Once over the stile and up the bank the back garden of Hog Wood Lodge is on the right. It contains a Type 29 pill box visible only in winter. Follow the turf strip footpath anti - clockwise round the headland of the field. It leads to a wooden stile into Hog Wood itself. You are on the 'friendly' side of SLG. Immediately over the stile on the right in the corner of the wood is a Type 26 pill box. Running parallel with the foot path through the wood is a section of unreinstated tank trap, Photograph 6. It gives a clear idea of the design and dimensions of this type of anti tank obstacle. Such length and good condition are found nowhere else on SLG. Where the wood thins to a double strip of trees there is a Type 29 pill box on the left and some partially refilled infantry trenches. They are the only ones surviving on SLG and are evidence that here at least there was defence with a little depth behind the anti tank obstacle. Another Type 29, in very good condition, is visible along the tank trap to the right, Photograph 12. The footpath continues to the gate at the far end of this narrow bit of wood.

Once through the gate turn left and cross the stile on the left just past the pond. Head for the corrugated iron roofed barn over two more stiles and following the yellow arrows take the path between the private gardens onto the tarmac lane through the hamlet of Pipehouse. Turn left on this lane then go through the gate on the left where the tarmac ends. On the far side of the field is the north edge of Hog Wood. Make for the right hand corner of it. From here Hog Wood Lodge is in sight again and the path crosses the field directly to it and the start point.

WHADDON, NEAR MELKSHAM, WILTSHIRE
Distance to walk : 3 miles
Ordnance Survey Map Sheet Explorer 156

Take the B3107 from Melksham to Bradford on Avon. A mile and a half from Melksham the road crosses the Chippenham to Bradford on Avon railway over a prominent hump back bridge. 300 yards after the bridge is a gravel and stone lay by on the left. On the opposite verge is a public foot path sign post. Park in the lay by and enter the gate indicated by the sign post. It is the start of a circuit past defence works 146 to 148 in Part Three and some substantial defence works of Stop Line Blue.

Head for the prominent white railway danger sign and cross the line by the stiles provided. Cross the next two narrow fields over the stone stile and the wooden stile. The River Avon, which is the anti tank obstacle at this point on SLG, is now visible. Half left is a red brick shuttered Type 29 pill box covering the stone Pack Horse Bridge over the river.

Cross the bridge and turn right following the river bank as far as the stone buttresses which used to support the bridge of the railway line between Devizes and Holt, in full use in 1940. This is the junction point of Stop Line Blue and Stop Line Green. On the far side of the river two Stop Line Green Type 29 pill boxes are visible, close in to the railway embankment. On top of the embankment on the walker's side of the river is a Stop Line Blue Type 29 pill box. The design is known as 'thin rear wall' because the rear wall is nothing like as thick as the other five. This reflects a touching faith that the enemy will not attack from the rear. Other construction differences are the high entrance door and the sloping edges of the roof. The defence works encountered from now on are all Stop Line Blue. Once past the railway bridge buttress an ornate wrought iron foot bridge over a River Avon tributary is visible half left over the next field. Cross this bridge and turn right up the steep bank to the Church of Saint Mary The Virgin. On the far side of the tarmac lane which runs past the church, underneath the power cables, is a Type 28 pill box. The anti tank gun firing port is bricked up, Photograph 10. Turn right on the lane and take the sharp left bend. At the end of the front garden hedge of the second house on the left is a collection of rectangular and tubular anti tank bollards. From this point a tank trap, long ago filled in, ran past the front of the Type 28 pill box already seen up to and beyond another Type 28 which will appear later in the walk. Continue along the lane. Where the farm buildings end on the right hand side there is a very large tubular anti tank bollard lying beside the hedge. When the lane crosses the Kennet Avon Canal turn left along the tow path and follow it to the next canal bridge. Scramble up the bank on the left immediately after the bridge and follow the raised foot path which becomes a hard surfaced track towards the grey stone farm, Whaddon Grove Farm. St Mary's Church and the Type 28 are again visible on the high ground half left. The second Type 28 pill box, also bricked up, is in the right hand corner of the front garden of Whaddon Grove Farm. On reaching the farm take the concrete road downhill to the stone bridge over the brook where there are tubular anti tank bollards on both verges. Half left at the base of the slurry lagoon wall is another thin rear wall Type 29 pill box covering the bridge. It is worth noting that Stop Line Blue at this point comprises three separate anti tank obstacles covered by fire from the various pill boxes - the canal, the tank trap and the tributary of the Avon. It is defence with a depth not seen on SLG which depends on a single anti tank obstacle covered by a single line of pill boxes. Stop Line Blue is built to face an enemy advancing from the direction of the canal. The 'friendly' side of SLG is on the west bank of the Avon, where the first pill box on the walk was passed. Cross the bridge and ascend the slight rise to the highest point leaving all the farm buildings on your right. The embankment of the Devizes to Holt railway line is again in sight. The footpath runs left handed through the cutting in the embankment. Once through this the Pack Horse Bridge is visible across the field on the left. The path goes directly to it. Cross the bridge and use the route from the parking place to return there.

LACKHAM, NEAR CHIPPENHAM, WILTSHIRE
Distance to walk : 3 miles
Ordnance Survey Map Sheet Explorer 156

Take the A350 from Chippenham to Melksham. One mile south of Chippenham the entrance to Lackham College of Agriculture is on the left. Just short of it on the right is a tarmac lay by in which to park. Walk through the College entrance to start a circuit past defence works 164 to 167 in Part Three, a Type 26 and 3 Type 29 pill boxes. The College drive rises to a high point then begins to descend. On the right is a red brick shuttered Type 29 pill box. It is both well made and dug in and is placed to face an enemy advancing up hill from the River Avon, the anti tank obstacle, which is beyond the College buildings at the foot of the hill. It is unusual on SLG in being sited so far back from and with no field of fire over the obstacle. There are more usually placed pill boxes within the Lackham grounds right on the river bank. Continue down hill to a grey chippings surfaced field entrance on the left with a stile beside the gate. Cross the stile and a public foot path runs beside the Avon towards the spire of St Paul's Church in Chippenham. Where the field now drops to the river on the right is a prefabricated shuttering Type 26 pill box,Photograph 1. It is also well dug in with an entrance stairway protected by blast walls on each side. Leaving the reed beds on the right cross the stile and foot bridge in the corner of the field. Cross the following four stiles then head for the prominent telegraph pole in the centre of the field. Leaving it on your right the next stile is visible, this time in a hedge rather than wire.

Before using this stile line yourself up with the large round post at the corner of the field on the right and the imposing white building on the horizon, Chippenham Magistrates Court. Between the post and the Courts a Type 29 pill box is visible on the bank of the Avon. Now cross the stile in the hedge, turn immediately left and cross another style in the hedge to your front. Turn left again and cross the next stile after which walk the headland of the field in a clockwise direction. In the thick hedge at the second field corner which you reach is another Type 29. It is dug in right up to the firing ports, is very well made, dry and still serviceable. It is set well back from the anti tank obstacle because the field in front of it is prone to flooding. Continue round the headland to the stile and cross into then out of the narrow strip of waste land via another stile and foot bridge over a deep ditch. Turn immediately left and follow the ditch back towards the Avon. The very high ground half right on the far side of the river is Bowden Hill noted in the 1940 military report on SLG, see Part Two. Rejoin the route used on the outward leg and follow it back to the parking place.

MALMESBURY, WILTSHIRE
Distance to walk : 2 and 1/2 miles
Ordnance Survey Map Sheet Explorer 168

Travel 1/2 mile south, that is towards Chippenham, from the roundabout junction of the A429 and B4040 on the Malmesbury by pass and park in the tarmac and paved lay by on the left. Where the paved section ends there is a stile in the post and rail fence on the left. Cross the stile and turn right on the stone track. You are on a circuit past defence works 183 to 187 in Part Three, a Type 26 and two Type 29 pill boxes, all made with prefabricated shuttering, a large cluster of anti tank bollards and some river bank revetting to improve the anti tank obstacle.

Follow the stone track to the junction with the tarmac lane and turn left over the cattle grid. Continue along the tarmac lane parallel with the River Avon. At the second electricity pole on the left look half right over the river up the hedge line of the field which runs right down to the river. Where the hedge merges with the wood is the Type 26 pill box. It is sited to cover both the Avon and the tank trap which ran down the field on the left and replaced the river as the anti tank obstacle at this point. The tank trap was filled in long ago in but there are detailed references to it in Part Two. Follow the tarmac lane until the railway bridge buttress of the old Malmesbury Branch Line, active in 1940, is on your left. On the far side of the river at this point the bank was faced with railway sleepers, Photograph 11. This defence work is called 'revetting' and is intended to make the bank vertical and impossible to climb by tanks which may have waded the river. Turn right along the path on top of the railway embankment. You are now on the 'enemy' side of both the river and the tank trap. Turn right off the embankment at the first field gate, cross the foot bridge over the Avon weir and turn left on the tarmac lane. Follow the lane to the junction with the B4042. Cow Bridge is on the immediate left. The plan in 1940 was to demolish this vital crossing point over the anti tank obstacle before the Germans reached it. There is a Type 29 pill box on the river bank in the spinney on the far,'enemy', side of the bridge. This is because military doctrine requires a physical presence between the enemy and the bridge so that they can not rush and capture it before the prepositioned explosive demolition charges have been fired.

Turn right up the pavement beside the B4042. After 50 yards cross the road and enter the field through the iron gate. The foot path follows the Avon on the bank of which is a group of 21 rectangular anti tank bollards. They blocked the exit from a ford over the river. The disadvantage of the bollards, noted by the family who farmed the field in 1940, is that they reveal the presence of the ford to an enemy who might not otherwise have discovered it. As the last bollard is reached turn right up the bank and right again along the hedge line to cross the stile and footbridge into the next field. A tennis court is now in sight and at the left end of it is another Type 29 with a fine field of fire onto Cow Bridge and the group of bollards. Turn left at the tennis court and cross the stile at the crest of the hill. The path now runs to the double power cable poles half right and thence downhill parallel with the private gardens to the A429.

Cross the A429, turn right and follow the pavement downhill through Parliament Row, cross the foot bridge over the Sherston Branch of the Avon, go through the wrought iron gates,turn left then immediately right into St John's Street. Follow St John's Street over the Tetbury Branch of the Avon (see Part Two), past the bowls club on the left and into Baskerville Lane. The confluence of the two branches of the Avon is on the right and Baskerville Lane runs parallel with the river to the cattle grid encountered on the first leg of the walk. Turn left to regain the parking place.

LONG NEWNTON, NEAR TETBURY, GLOUCESTERSHIRE
Distance to walk : 3 and a 1/2 miles -
Ordnance Survey Map Sheet Explorer 168

Take the B4014 from Tetbury to Malmesbury. You will pass through Long
Newnton where the road dips through the village then rises to a sweeping
right hand bend with a stand of trees on a triangle of grass and two
converging side roads on the left. Park on the tarmac behind the triangle and
walk up the lane signed dead end. You are on a circuit past defence works
198 to 204 in Part Three, a prefabricated shuttering Type 26 pill box, 5 red
brick shuttered Type 29 pill boxes and a length of tank trap hump.

Follow the foot path arrows right handed and through the wrought iron stile.
Pass the ruined barn on the left and take the turf track along the headland of
the field with the Cotswold stone boundary wall and Newnton Manor House
on your right. A substantial corrugated iron barn appears across the field on
the right and on the near crest half right over the valley the Type 26 pill box is
set in a stone wall, Photograph 2. Go through the gate when the wall beside
the turf track ends and turn left on the raised turf track. It is raised because it
is the hump of the carelessly reinstated tank trap which was the anti tank
obstacle at this point on SLG. On the right of the first gate you reach walking
along the hump is a Type 29 pill box. Go straight through the gate and walk
the headland of the next three fields keeping close to the hedge at your left
hand. The high ground on your right was Long Newton Aerodrome which
was a Flying Training School in the Great War and a decoy airfield in the
Second War intended to attract German bombers away from nearby
operational stations such as Aston Down. It was on the 'enemy' side of SLG.
Follow the finger posts straight over the tarmac lane which you reach,
Crudwell Lane,and take the stone track. The derelict buildings on either side
of the track were part of the aerodrome. Continue along the track until it
divides left and right at the corner of the large wood, Addy's Firs. Turn left
and follow the headland with Addy's Firs on your right and when the trees
end another Type 29 is to your front in the corner of the field. It is well dug in
and in good condition. Go through the gate on the right of the pill box and
follow the foot path arrows along the turf strip over the next two fields to the
tarmac lane. As you cross the first field the third Type 29 is in the far right
hand corner, it is only visible during winter. As you cross the second field the
fourth is similarly placed but as it is at the road side can be easily visited by
turning right on the lane. To continue the walk turn left on the lane then take
the first left,you are back on Crudwell Lane. The road dips steeply then rises
and descends past the fifth Type 29 pill box in the bushes on the right verge.
You will cross the route followed on the outward section of the walk and
should use it to return to the parking place.

AVENING, NEAR TETBURY, GLOUCESTERSHIRE
Distance to walk : 1 and a 1/2 miles
Ordnance Survey Map Sheet Explorer 168

Take the B4014 from Tetbury to Avening. 1 and 1/2 miles after the built up area of Tetbury ends is a cross roads at which you turn right. 1 mile later Star Farm is on the right opposite a T junction which you go straight past. Park on the open hard area on the right 400 yards further on just short of the cross roads formed by a bridle path on the left and a tarmac lane on the right. Walk down the bridle path and you are on a circuit past defence works 212 to 216 in Part Three. They are 2 prefabricated shuttering Type 29 pill boxes, a length of unreinstated tank trap, a length of tank trap hump and some anti tank bollards. The tank trap ran all the way from Avening until it joined the River Avon at Malmesbury (see Part Two).

As you pass the triangular pine wood on the left of the bridle path the first Type 29 is across the field on the left in front of the terraced cottages. It is placed to face an enemy from the direction of the bridle path. Continue along the bridle path then cross the stone stile on the left just short of the electricity line. Go straight over the field and cross the stone stile in the wall. Immediately before you is a vivid example of the uncultivable tank trap hump, Photograph 7. The War Office laughably classified this as 'reinstated' but it is of no more use to the farmer than a rock garden. Turn right down the hump,go through the gate and turn right on the stone track. Look left over the wall beside the track where the hump continues to the crest. This was the start of the continuous Avening to Malmesbury tank trap. Take the almost immediate sharp left on the stone track down the steep hill to the tarmac lane and turn left again. Just before the junction of this lane with the main road is a Gloucestershire County Council foot path finger post to direct you up the steep bank on the left and through the iron gate into the field. The second Type 29 pill box is visible half left below the crest at the start of the tank trap. Climb the field and cross the stone stile in front of the houses into the tarmac lane,Star Lane,then turn left up the hill. 50 yards before the sharp right hand bend 4 ivy covered tubular anti tank bollards are set into the bank on the right. Once past the bollards you are on the 'friendly' side of SLG. Continue up Star Lane past the field with the prominent tank trap hump and the first Type 29, now both on the left,then turn left at the T junction in front of Star Farm. Starting just beyond the Star Farm buildings there is a strip wood on the right verge of the lane as far as the parking place. Running through it parallel with the lane is the length of unreinstated tank trap. It is used to store rolls of sheep netting and is very overgrown. It is best seen by scrambling into the strip wood, half way along it, from the lane. The dimensions and the very stony ground in which it was dug are then apparent.

UPPER FRAMILODE, NEAR STROUD, GLOUCESTERSHIRE
Distance to walk : 3 and a 1/2 miles -
Ordnance Survey Map Sheet Outdoor Leisure 14

Take the B4071 from the junction with the A38 through Frampton on Severn,over the Sharpness Canal and through the village of Saul. Leave Saul on Moor Street and an elaborate metal foot bridge appears on the right giving access to an electricity transformer. Park at the entrance to the foot bridge. Walk on past the first few villas of Upper Framilode on the right to the red brick bridge over the Stroud Water Canal, the designated anti tank obstacle, see Part Two. Cross the bridge and turn right down the canal tow path. You are now on a circuit past defence works 221 to 223 in Part Three, 3 prefabricated shuttering pill boxes.

As you cross the first stile look hard left across the River Frome beside you. On the far side of the Frome is a Type 29 pill box. It is sited with a field of fire back towards Saul which is completely the wrong direction, Saul being on the 'friendly' side of the canal. It can not even cover the road bridge over the Frome in Upper Framilode which would have been a useful function. Similar peculiar sitings are found elsewhere on SLG, Photograph 13. They are errors by the local firms contracted to build the pill boxes. Follow the foot path markers over the stiles and through the gates provided along the raised path with the Frome on your left. The path is the Stroud Water Canal tow path. The canal, filled in here,was on your right. As you reach the Sharpness Canal at Junction Bridge the Wycliffe College Rowing Club is on the left and just beyond it there is a Type 26 pill box on the tow path. Cross the Sharpness canal by the foot bridge, turn immediately left in front of Junction Bridge House then right over the stile beside the canal traffic lights. Head for the tower of St Andrew's Church across the field. The foot path runs beside the red brick walled garden of Whitminster House on the right, through a kissing gate beneath the Yew trees into the church yard,past the church on the left,out of the church yard through another kissing gate and straight on to a wrought iron stile into the Whitminster to Frampton lane. Cross the lane and follow the foot path markers along the turf track over three fields then turn right on the hard track leaving the red brick cottage on the left. Turn right again at the junction with the next hard track and cross the Stroud Water Canal on Stonepits Bridge. Turn right along the bank and a Type 26 pill box is beside the canal. Follow the track past it, cross the stone bridge over the River Frome then the stile on the right to follow the path beside that river. Once through the river bank strip wood the Stroud Water Canal reappears on the left. Follow the canal, keeping it on your left, from the restored lock beside the Frome weir system, over the Whitminster to Frampton lane at Walk Bridge, thence along the tow path back to Junction Bridge. Once past Walk Bridge the Stroud Water is still in pristine condition and as good an anti tank obstacle as the 1940 planners took it to be. However, no armoured commander would willingly advance through this Severn Vale country of small enclosures, soft ground, deep ditches and frequent water courses. From Junction Bridge use the route from the parking place to return to it.

Photo No.13 Type 29 pill box at Freshford sited for extra protection against bombs but with a tiny field of fire.